MW00895256

TO WHOM IT MAY CONCERN

LETTER *from a* RAPTURED SOUL

TO WHOM IT MAY CONCERN

DAWN LEWIS

Maranatha
Dawn Lewis

xulon
PRESS

Copyright © 2014 by Dawn Lewis

TO WHOM IT MAY CONCERN
LETTER from a RAPTURED SOUL
by Dawn Lewis

Printed in the United States of America

ISBN 9781498413336

All rights reserved solely by the author. The author guarantees all contents are original and do not infringe upon the legal rights of any other person or work. No part of this book may be reproduced in any form without the permission of the author. The views expressed in this book are not necessarily those of the publisher.

Scripture quotations taken from the King James Version (KJV) – public domain

www.xulonpress.com

TO WHOM IT MAY CONCERN...

Throughout my life I ran from God
Searching for something unknown.
After all my running was done I found
With Him I was finally whole.

You have run, too, but now running is through—
A choice you must now make.
Jesus Christ has come, and with Him I've gone home;
But you didn't, and now your soul is at stake.

He asked me once to write it all—
The trials and tests to come.
In this way you would know who to trust
And who you should flee from.

He also said this would be left
But not without a reason,
Because He would soon be coming back
And someone would need it in due season.

You are the reason it has all been written,
So that finally to Him you would turn.
And so I write this down for you...
To Whom It May Concern.

People who are *concerned* in any measure about the ways and things of God read His Word. They not only read it, but study His Word and hide it in their hearts.

- Concerned about their salvation
- Concerned about the truth
- Concerned about the future
- Concerned about where their soul or the souls of their loved ones will spend eternity
- Concerned about how to go to Heaven *and* not end up *there* (the other place)

So I have written the "dedication" as I believe He has inspired me to write it...

To Whom It May Concern

First, let me say that this book is not to take the place of the Bible. If you can get your hands on one–*do it now!* Read it, hide the Word in your heart and share the Word with everyone you know as quickly as you can.

This book contains the testimony of one who *believed* and is now *gone.* It has been left by someone who cares about your soul to help you to understand what has happened and what will happen—plain and simple.

It is akin to a Last Will and Testament in that you are inheriting the testimony of one who has "gone on", except I'm not dead and neither is the person who has left their testimony in this book. We have simply gone home to heaven with the Lord. We've been raptured, taken in the twinkling of an eye.

Maybe we were alone when He called us, when the trumpet sounded, or maybe we were with someone like the Book of Matthew states:

Matthew 24

[36]But of that day and hour knoweth no man, no, not the angels of heaven, but my Father only.

[37]But as the days of Noah were, so shall also the coming of the Son of man be.

[38]For as in the days that were before the flood they were eating and drinking, marrying and giving in marriage, until the day that Noah entered into the ark,

[39]And knew not until the flood came, and took them all away; so shall also the coming of the Son of man be.

[40]Then shall two be in the field; the one shall be taken, and the other left. (That is what has happened.)

[41]Two women shall be grinding at the mill; the one shall be taken, and the other left.

[42]Watch therefore: for ye know not what hour your Lord doth come.

There is much to be told over the next few pages, most you may not believe. But by comparing the "signs of the times" as they have been called, I pray that you will soon come to believe it all. *This is the last chance you have.*

I must tell you now that you have missed the most important invitation in your life. The invitation to the Marriage Supper of my Lord, Jesus Christ! That is where we are now. I don't know why you are still here. Except for the grace of God and the redeeming, sin-cleansing blood of Jesus Christ, I would be here, too. There is *nothing* else that would have kept me from being "left behind" like you.

Ephesians 2

[8]For by grace are ye saved through faith; and that not of yourselves: it is the gift of God:

[9]Not of works, lest any man should boast.

This is Matthew's full account of what Jesus himself had to say about the time of His Return:

Matthew 24

[1]And Jesus went out, and departed from the temple: and his disciples came to him for to shew him the buildings of the temple.

[2]And Jesus said unto them, See ye not all these things? verily I say unto you, There shall not be left here one stone upon another, that shall not be thrown down.

[3]And as he sat upon the mount of Olives, the disciples came unto him privately, saying, Tell us, when shall these things be? and what shall be the sign of thy coming, and of the end of the world?

[4]And Jesus answered and said unto them, Take heed that no man deceive you.

[5]For many shall come in my name, saying, I am Christ; and shall deceive many.

[6]And ye shall hear of wars and rumours of wars: see that ye be not troubled: for all these things must come to pass, but the end is not yet.

[7]For nation shall rise against nation, and kingdom against kingdom: and there shall be famines, and pestilences, and earthquakes, in divers places.

[8]All these are the beginning of sorrows.

[9]Then shall they deliver you up to be afflicted, and shall kill you: and ye shall be hated of all nations for my name's sake.

[10]And then shall many be offended, and shall betray one another, and shall hate one another.

[11]And many false prophets shall rise, and shall deceive many.

[12]And because iniquity shall abound, the love of many shall wax cold.

[13]But he that shall endure unto the end, the same shall be saved.

[14]And this gospel of the kingdom shall be preached in all the world for a witness unto all nations; and then shall the end come.

[15]When ye therefore shall see the abomination of desolation, spoken of by Daniel the prophet, stand in the holy place, (whoso readeth, let him understand:)

[16]Then let them which be in Judaea flee into the mountains:

[17]Let him which is on the housetop not come down to take any thing out of his house:

[18]Neither let him which is in the field return back to take his clothes.

[19]And woe unto them that are with child, and to them that give suck in those days!

[20]But pray ye that your flight be not in the winter, neither on the sabbath day:

[21]For then shall be great tribulation, such as was not since the beginning of the world to this time, no, nor ever shall be.

[22]And except those days should be shortened, there should no flesh be saved: but for the elect's sake those days shall be shortened.

[23]Then if any man shall say unto you, Lo, here is Christ, or there; believe it not.

[24]For there shall arise false Christs, and false prophets, and shall shew great signs and wonders; insomuch that, if it were possible, they shall deceive the very elect.

[25]Behold, I have told you before.

[26]Wherefore if they shall say unto you, Behold, he is in the desert; go not forth: behold, he is in the secret chambers; believe it not.

[27]For as the lightning cometh out of the east, and shineth even unto the west; so shall also the coming of the Son of man be.

[28]For wheresoever the carcase is, there will the eagles be gathered together.

[29]Immediately after the tribulation of those days shall the sun be darkened, and the moon shall not give her light, and the stars shall fall from heaven, and the powers of the heavens shall be shaken:

[30]And then shall appear the sign of the Son of man in heaven: and then shall all the tribes of the earth mourn, and they shall see the Son of man coming in the clouds of heaven with power and great glory.

[31]And he shall send his angels with a great sound of a trumpet, and they shall gather together his elect from the four winds, from one end of heaven to the other.

[32]Now learn a parable of the fig tree; When his branch is yet tender, and putteth forth leaves, ye know that summer is nigh:

[33]So likewise ye, when ye shall see all these things, know that it is near, even at the doors.

[34]Verily I say unto you, This generation shall not pass, till all these things be fulfilled.

[35]Heaven and earth shall pass away, but my words shall not pass away.

[36]But of that day and hour knoweth no man, no, not the angels of heaven, but my Father only.

[37]But as the days of Noah were, so shall also the coming of the Son of man be.

[38]For as in the days that were before the flood they were eating and drinking, marrying and giving in marriage, until the day that Noe entered into the ark,

[39]And knew not until the flood came, and took them all away; so shall also the coming of the Son of man be.

[40]Then shall two be in the field; the one shall be taken, and the other left.

[41]Two women shall be grinding at the mill; the one shall be taken, and the other left.

[42]Watch therefore: for ye know not what hour your Lord doth come.

[43]But know this, that if the goodman of the house had known in what watch the thief would come, he would have watched, and would not have suffered his house to be broken up.

[44]Therefore be ye also ready: for in such an hour as ye think not the Son of man cometh.

[45]Who then is a faithful and wise servant, whom his lord hath made ruler over his household, to give them meat in due season?

[46]Blessed is that servant, whom his lord when he cometh shall find so doing.

[47]Verily I say unto you, That he shall make him ruler over all his goods.

[48]But and if that evil servant shall say in his heart, My lord delayeth his coming;

[49]And shall begin to smite his fellowservants, and to eat and drink with the drunken;

[50]The lord of that servant shall come in a day when he looketh not for him, and in an hour that he is not aware of,

[51]And shall cut him asunder, and appoint him his portion with the hypocrites: there shall be weeping and gnashing of teeth.

This is Mark's witness for the words Jesus spoke:

Mark 13

[1]And as he went out of the temple, one of his disciples saith unto him, Master, see what manner of stones and what buildings are here!

[2]And Jesus answering said unto him, Seest thou these great buildings? there shall not be left one stone upon another, that shall not be thrown down.

[3]And as he sat upon the mount of Olives over against the temple, Peter and James and John and Andrew asked him privately,

[4]Tell us, when shall these things be? and what shall be the sign when all these things shall be fulfilled?

[5]And Jesus answering them began to say, Take heed lest any man deceive you:

[6]For many shall come in my name, saying, I am Christ; and shall deceive many.

[7]And when ye shall hear of wars and rumours of wars, be ye not troubled: for such things must needs be; but the end shall not be yet.

[8]For nation shall rise against nation, and kingdom against kingdom: and there shall be earthquakes in divers places, and there shall be famines and troubles: these are the beginnings of sorrows.

[9]But take heed to yourselves: for they shall deliver you up to councils; and in the synagogues ye shall be beaten: and ye shall be brought before

rulers and kings for my sake, for a testimony against them.

[10]And the gospel must first be published among all nations.

[11]But when they shall lead you, and deliver you up, take no thought beforehand what ye shall speak, neither do ye premeditate: but whatsoever shall be given you in that hour that speak ye: for it is not ye that speak, but the Holy Ghost.

[12]Now the brother shall betray the brother to death, and the father the son; and children shall rise up against their parents, and shall cause them to be put to death.

[13]And ye shall be hated of all men for my name's sake: but he that shall endure unto the end, the same shall be saved.

[14]But when ye shall see the abomination of desolation, spoken of by Daniel the prophet, standing where it ought not, (let him that readeth understand,) then let them that be in Judaea flee to the mountains:

[15]And let him that is on the housetop not go down into the house, neither enter therein, to take any thing out of his house:

[16]And let him that is in the field not turn back again for to take up his garment.

[17]But woe to them that are with child, and to them that give suck in those days!

[18]And pray ye that your flight be not in the winter.

[19]For in those days shall be affliction, such as was not from the beginning of the creation which God created unto this time, neither shall be.

[20]And except that the Lord had shortened those days, no flesh should be saved: but for the elect's sake, whom he hath chosen, he hath shortened the days.

[21]And then if any man shall say to you, Lo, here is Christ; or, lo, he is there; believe him not:

[22]For false Christs and false prophets shall rise, and shall shew signs and wonders, to seduce, if it were possible, even the elect.

[23] But take ye heed: behold, I have foretold you all things.

[24]But in those days, after that tribulation, the sun shall be darkened, and the moon shall not give her light,

[25]And the stars of heaven shall fall, and the powers that are in heaven shall be shaken.

[26]And then shall they see the Son of man coming in the clouds with great power and glory.

[27]And then shall he send his angels, and shall gather together his elect from the four winds, from the uttermost part of the earth to the uttermost part of heaven.

[28]Now learn a parable of the fig tree; When her branch is yet tender, and putteth forth leaves, ye know that summer is near:

[29]So ye in like manner, when ye shall see these things come to pass, know that it is nigh, even at the doors.

[30]Verily I say unto you, that this generation shall not pass, till all these things be done.

[31]Heaven and earth shall pass away: but my words shall not pass away.

[32]But of that day and that hour knoweth no man, no, not the angels which are in heaven, neither the Son, but the Father.

[33]Take ye heed, watch and pray: for ye know not when the time is.

[34]For the Son of Man is as a man taking a far journey, who left his house, and gave authority to his servants, and to every man his work, and commanded the porter to watch.

[35]Watch ye therefore: for ye know not when the master of the house cometh, at even, or at midnight, or at the cockcrowing, or in the morning:

[36]Lest coming suddenly he find you sleeping.

[37]And what I say unto you I say unto all, Watch.

I don't know at what point of the seven year (yes, seven year) Tribulation period you have found this, so the information in this book, or what you have to look forward to, will be written as if the Rapture, or the taking up of the church, has just taken place. One thing you have probably realized, or will shortly, is that "life" on Earth has suddenly become different.

If you had heard anything about the Rapture prior to its occurrence, you may know that it has indeed taken place. Oh, I know that the government heads, news media and maybe even friends and family may have tried very hard to explain it all away. Many people may even be convinced by their explanations of mass hysteria, aliens, spontaneous combustion even. *Ha!* But be not deceived any longer. Jesus Christ himself has returned for His Bride, the Church, and we are now with Him!

It doesn't matter that your friends or family may be here with you, acting and living as if nothing has happened. They are under the power of deception; a power that you will have to fight, and possibly deny to your death, if you finally intend to stand with Jesus Christ. This will be *impossible to do on your own.* Prior to this day you may not have become a Christian before because it was too hard, or you were afraid of ridicule or embarrassment. You ain't seen nothin' yet!

In the Bible, 1 Thessalonians 5 describes our sudden departure this way:

> ²For yourselves know perfectly that the day of the Lord so cometh as a thief in the night.

And other verses in Thessalonians say:

1 Thessalonians 4

> ¹⁶For the Lord himself shall descend from heaven with a shout, with the voice of the archangel, and with the trump of God: and the dead in Christ shall rise first:

[17]Then we which are alive and remain shall be caught up together with them in the clouds, to meet the Lord in the air: and so shall we ever be with the Lord.

You were deceived in the past and that is why you're still here. Still don't believe a *great number* of people are "missing"? Look at the evidence for yourself; cars wrecked without drivers, babies and children missing, empty houses that look as if their owners stepped out to check the mail. Maybe someone you knew or were close to is gone without a trace.

If the Rapture (yes, I'll keep saying it, since it is what it is) hasn't just taken place, maybe a little time has passed, maybe things haven't been so bad after all. Maybe you have had some time to "adjust" to this new world. Since the Rapture there have not been any Christians knocking on your door for you to worry about. And that person that you used to work with who was some how "different" from everyone else doesn't bug you about visiting their church or going to a Bible study.

No longer do you have to flip channels on a Sunday morning to find something worth watching, because there are nothing but "Bible-thumpers" on. No more do you have to hear your grandmother say, "I love you and I'm praying for you." *We are gone!*

Before the Rapture you may have considered giving your heart and life to Jesus. But you felt that you would be giving up more than you would get.

You probably thought that being a Christian was very difficult and maybe not even worth it—whatever "it" is or was. So here you are. You've been lured, lied to, and cheated. You have gained the world, and possibly lost your soul in the process. Was all this worth staying behind for? Can your answer be anything but "*No*"?

Ok, well sure you have decided to stay here. After all, that was the *choice* you made. Let me tell you what you have to look forward to. First off, look at who is in charge of the world, or at least getting the most attention at this point. There is going to be someone that the Bible refers to as the Antichrist who will come forward with the solution to everyone's problems, and oh, peace at last for Israel.

This will be your big clue as to who this person is, what they represent, and who not to trust or follow. He will be the person most instrumental in bringing forth a peace agreement for, and possibly with, Israel. And *finally,* there will be "Peace on Earth."

Looking around, things may seem almost "normal"—but beware. All "hell" is going to break loose literally.

God's angels and the presence of His people are no longer holding back the forces that have tried to rule the Earth, the judgments from God Himself *are just beginning*, and there isn't a Christian that you can turn to.

You may have finally come to realize that you are, in all reality–

ALONE!

Just when you think life may be better after all, and you might be OK, now is when the *fun* starts…

Following are the occurrences listed in the sixth chapter of the Book of Revelation, or John's vision, that you may personally experience. Soon judgments will begin to be released on the Earth from the Lamb of God, Jesus Himself, as He opens a scroll sealed with seven seals. Seven Seal Judgments and Seven Trumpet Judgments will be released one by one over the first 3 ½ year period of the Tribulation.

The First Seal: A Rider on a White Horse

Possibly the Antichrist

Revelation 6

¹And I saw when the Lamb opened one of the seals, and I heard, as it were, the noise of

thunder, one of the four beasts saying, "Come and see." [2]And I saw, and behold a white horse: and he that sat on him had a bow; and a crown was given unto him: and he went forth conquering, and to conquer.

The Second Seal: A Rider on a Red Horse

Possibly representing the blood spilled from war on earth

[3]And when he had opened the second seal, I heard the second beast say, "Come and see." [4]And there went out another horse that was red: and power was given to him that sat thereon to take peace from the earth, and that they should kill one another: and there was given unto him a great sword.

The Third Seal: A Rider on a Black Horse

Representing famine

[5]And when he had opened the third seal, I heard the third beast say, "Come and see." And I beheld, and lo a black horse; and he that sat on him had a pair of balances in his hand. [6]And I heard a voice in the midst of the four beasts say, "A measure of wheat for a penny, and three measures of barley for a penny; and see thou hurt not the oil and the wine."

The Fourth Seal: A Rider on a Green Horse

As a result of warfare, famine, and disease, one-fourth of the world's population dies

> [7]And when he had opened the fourth seal, I heard the voice of the fourth beast say, "Come and see." [8]And I looked, and behold a pale horse: and his name that sat on him was Death, and Hell followed with him. And power was given unto them over the fourth part of the earth, to kill with sword, and with hunger, and with death, and with the beasts of the earth.

The Fifth Seal: Souls Under the Altar

These are the souls of those who were martyred for the sake of Christ before the Rapture

> [9]And when he had opened the fifth seal, I saw under the altar the souls of them that were slain for the word of God, and for the testimony which they held: [10]And they cried with a loud voice, saying, "How long, O Lord, holy and true, dost thou not judge and avenge our blood on them that dwell on the earth?" [11]And white robes were given unto every one of them; and it was said unto them, that they should rest yet for a little season, until their fellowservants also and their brethren, that should be killed as they were, should be fulfilled.

The Sixth Seal: Natural Disasters

People will hide in caves and mountains from fear of all that is taking place around them

[12]And I beheld when he had opened the sixth seal, and, lo, there was a great earthquake; and the sun became black as sackcloth of hair, and the moon became as blood; [13]And the stars of heaven fell unto the earth, even as a fig tree casteth her untimely figs, when she is shaken of a mighty wind. [14]And the heaven departed as a scroll when it is rolled together; and every mountain and island were moved out of their places.

[15]And the kings of the earth, and the great men, and the rich men, and the chief captains, and the mighty men, and every bondman, and every free man, hid themselves in the dens and in the rocks of the mountains; [16]And said to the mountains and rocks, "Fall on us, and hide us from the face of him that sitteth on the throne, and from the wrath of the Lamb: [17]For the great day of his wrath is come; and who shall be able to stand?"

The Seventh Seal: Silence in Heaven

Revelation 8

[1]And when he had opened the seventh seal, there was silence in heaven about the space of half an hour.

Now the Trumpet Judgments begin:

THE TRUMPET JUDGMENTS

[2]And I saw the seven angels which stood before God; and to them were given seven trumpets.

[3]And another angel came and stood at the altar, having a golden censer; and there was given unto him much incense, that he should offer it with the prayers of all saints upon the golden altar which was before the throne.

The First Trumpet: Hail and Fire with Blood

One-third of the earth's vegetation will be destroyed

[7]The first angel sounded, and there followed hail and fire mingled with blood, and they were cast upon the earth: and the third part of trees was burnt up, and all green grass was burnt up.

The Second Trumpet: A Burning Mountain Falls from the Sky to the Sea

One-third of the sea turns to blood; one-third of the sea creatures die: one-third of all the ships are destroyed

[8]And the second angel sounded, and as it were a great mountain burning with fire was cast into the sea: and the third part of the sea became blood;

[9]And the third part of the creatures which were in the sea, and had life, died; and the third part of the ships were destroyed.

The Third Trumpet: A Great Star Falls from Heaven

One-third of drinking water becomes contaminated and causes many to die from poisoning

[10]And the third angel sounded, and there fell a great star from heaven, burning as it were a lamp, and it fell upon the third part of the rivers, and upon the fountains of waters;

[11]And the name of the star is called Wormwood: and the third part of the waters became wormwood; and many men died of the waters, because they were made bitter.

The Fourth Trumpet: One-third of Earth's Light is Darkened

[12]And the fourth angel sounded, and the third part of the sun was smitten, and the third part of the moon, and the third part of the stars; so as the third part of them was darkened, and the day shone not for a third part of it, and the night likewise.

[13]And I beheld, and heard an angel flying through the midst of heaven, saying with a loud voice, "Woe, woe, woe, to the inhabiters of the earth by reason of the other voices of the trumpet of the three angels, which are yet to sound!"

The Fifth Trumpet: The Attack of the Poisonous Locusts

For five months people will suffer painful torture

Revelation 9

[1]And the fifth angel sounded, and I saw a star fall from heaven unto the earth: and to him was given the key of the bottomless pit.

[2]And he opened the bottomless pit; and there arose a smoke out of the pit, as the smoke of a great furnace; and the sun and the air were darkened by reason of the smoke of the pit.

[3]And there came out of the smoke locusts upon the earth: and unto them was given power, as the scorpions of the earth have power.

[4]And it was commanded them that they should not hurt the grass of the earth, neither any green thing, neither any tree; but only those men which have not the seal of God in their foreheads.

[5]And to them it was given that they should not kill them, but that they should be tormented five months: and their torment was as the torment of a scorpion, when he striketh a man.

[6]And in those days shall men seek death, and shall not find it; and shall desire to die, and death shall flee from them.

[7]And the shapes of the locusts were like unto horses prepared unto battle; and on their heads were as it were crowns like gold, and their faces were as the faces of men.

[8]And they had hair as the hair of women, and their teeth were as the teeth of lions.

[9]And they had breastplates, as it were breastplates of iron; and the sound of their wings was as the sound of chariots of many horses running to battle.

[10]And they had tails like unto scorpions, and there were stings in their tails: and their power was to hurt men five months.

[11]And they had a king over them, which is the angel of the bottomless pit, whose name in the Hebrew tongue is Abaddon, but in the Greek tongue hath his name Apollyon.

[12]One woe is past; and, behold, there come two woes more hereafter.

The Sixth Trumpet: The Attack of Two Hundred Million Horsemen

One-third of the remaining number of people are killed

[13]And the sixth angel sounded, and I heard a voice from the four horns of the golden altar which is before God,

[14]Saying to the sixth angel which had the trumpet, Loose the four angels which are bound in the great river Euphrates.

[15]And the four angels were loosed, which were prepared for an hour, and a day, and a month, and a year, for to slay the third part of men.

[16]And the number of the army of the horsemen were two hundred thousand thousand: and I heard the number of them.

[17]And thus I saw the horses in the vision, and them that sat on them, having breastplates of fire, and of jacinth, and brimstone: and the heads of the horses were as the heads of lions; and out of their mouths issued fire and smoke and brimstone.

[18]By these three was the third part of men killed, by the fire, and by the smoke, and by the brimstone, which issued out of their mouths.

[19]For their power is in their mouth, and in their tails: for their tails were like unto serpents, and had heads, and with them they do hurt.

[20]And the rest of the men which were not killed by these plagues yet repented not of the works of their hands, that they should not worship devils, and idols of gold, and silver, and brass, and stone, and of wood: which neither can see, nor hear, nor walk:

[21]Neither repented they of their murders, nor of their sorceries, nor of their fornication, nor of their thefts.

The Seventh Trumpet: Two Witnesses, a Great Earthquake, and the Elders Worship God in Heaven

Revelation 11

[14]The second woe is past; and, behold, the third woe cometh quickly.

[15]And the seventh angel sounded; and there were great voices in heaven, saying, The kingdoms of this world are become the kingdoms of our

Lord, and of his Christ; and he shall reign for ever and ever.

[16]And the four and twenty elders, which sat before God on their seats, fell upon their faces, and worshipped God,

[17]Saying, We give thee thanks, O LORD God Almighty, which art, and wast, and art to come; because thou hast taken to thee thy great power, and hast reigned.

[18]And the nations were angry, and thy wrath is come, and the time of the dead, that they should be judged, and that thou shouldest give reward unto thy servants the prophets, and to the saints, and them that fear thy name, small and great; and shouldest destroy them which destroy the earth.

[19]And the temple of God was opened in heaven, and there was seen in his temple the ark of his testament: and there were lightnings, and voices, and thunderings, and an earthquake, and great hail.

All of these things will occur in the first 3 ½ years of the seven-year Tribulation period. There will be approximately 3½ years of man-made "peace"—if you can call everything that has happened so far as *peaceful*. After that, and maybe sooner, the pressure will be on to finish the work that was started in the Garden of Eden: the deception and destruction of man, and the battle for souls—your soul.

It may be about this time that, since the "cat is out of the bag," this Antichrist person is going to start demanding a little *loyalty*. The Antichrist (Satan's little puppet) will do what he does best—show himself as the liar and deceiver that he is; "peace" will come to an end.

Revelation 13

¹And I stood upon the sand of the sea, and saw a beast rise up out of the sea, having seven heads and ten horns, and upon his horns ten crowns, and upon his heads the name of blasphemy. ²And the beast which I saw was like unto a leopard, and his feet were as the feet of a bear, and his mouth as the mouth of a lion: and the dragon gave him his power, and his seat, and great authority. ³And I saw one of his heads as it were wounded to death; and his deadly wound was healed: and all the world wondered after the beast. ⁴And they worshipped the dragon which gave power unto the beast: and they worshipped the beast, saying, Who is like unto the beast? who is able to make war with him?

⁵And there was given unto him a mouth speaking great things and blasphemies; and power was given unto him to continue forty and two months. ⁶And he opened his mouth in blasphemy against God, to blaspheme his name, and his tabernacle, and them that dwell in heaven. ⁷And it was given unto him to make war with the saints, and to overcome them: and power was given him over all kindreds, and tongues, and nations. ⁸And all that dwell upon the earth shall worship him, whose names are not written in the book of life of the Lamb slain from the foundation of the world.

[9]If any man have an ear, let him hear. [10]He that leadeth into captivity shall go into captivity: he that killeth with the sword must be killed with the sword. Here is the patience and the faith of the saints.

[11]And I beheld another beast coming up out of the earth; and he had two horns like a lamb, and he spake as a dragon. [12]And he exerciseth all the power of the first beast before him, and causeth the earth and them which dwell therein to worship the first beast, whose deadly wound was healed. [13]And he doeth great wonders, so that he maketh fire come down from heaven on the earth in the sight of men,

[14]And deceiveth them that dwell on the earth by the means of those miracles which he had power to do in the sight of the beast; saying to them that dwell on the earth, that they should make an image to the beast, which had the wound by a sword, and did live. [15]And he had power to give life unto the image of the beast, that the image of the beast should both speak, and cause that as many as would not worship the image of the beast should be killed. [16]And he causeth all, both small and great, rich and poor, free and bond, to receive a mark in their right hand, or in their foreheads: [17]And that no man might buy or sell, save he that had the mark, or the name of the beast, or the number of his name.

[18]Here is wisdom. Let him that hath understanding count the number of the beast: for it is the number of a man; and his number is Six hundred threescore and six.

Without this "mark" you will not be allowed to buy or sell anything. Anyone with the mark caught buying and selling to someone without the mark will probably be put to death immediately. What is this mark, and how could it be accomplished? Well, look around. The technology may already be in place—if not, surely it is under development.

We love convenience, but at what cost? Think about the debit card and the little keychain fob that allows purchases to be made with a wave of your hand. And even further, we now can ID our pets with a little chip the size of a grain of rice implanted under their skin…which is also being used in people! This may not be the actual type of ID or method used, *but the technology is here!*

You may give in and take the mark so that you are not killed, or maybe so that one of your family members or friends is not harmed, and that may end the pressures for now. But be aware of this: "they" may leave you alone because you are one of them, but your problems will only have just begun—and these will last for an eternity.

Revelation 14

[11]And the smoke of their torment ascendeth up for ever and ever: and they have no rest day nor night, who worship the beast and his image, and whosoever receiveth the mark of his name.

While this is going on, more judgments begin to be released:

THE SEVEN BOWL JUDGMENTS

Revelation 15

[1]And I saw another sign in heaven, great and marvellous, seven angels having the seven last plagues; for in them is filled up the wrath of God.

The First Bowl

Anyone who has taken the mark of the beast or worshipped his statue will break out with horrible sores

Revelation 16

[1]And I heard a great voice out of the temple saying to the seven angels, Go your ways, and pour out the vials of the wrath of God upon the earth.

[2]And the first went, and poured out his vial upon the earth; and there fell a noisome and grievous sore upon the men which had the mark of the beast, and upon them which worshipped his image.

The Second Bowl

The oceans all turn to blood and anything left alive in them to this point dies

[3]And the second angel poured out his vial upon the sea; and it became as the blood of a dead man: and every living soul died in the sea.

The Third Bowl

The rivers and the springs of earth turn to blood as well

[4]And the third angel poured out his vial upon the rivers and fountains of waters; and they became blood.

[5]And I heard the angel of the waters say, Thou art righteous, O Lord, which art, and wast, and shalt be, because thou hast judged thus.

[6]For they have shed the blood of saints and prophets, and thou hast given them blood to drink; for they are worthy.

[7]And I heard another out of the altar say, "Even so, Lord God Almighty, true and righteous are thy judgments."

The Fourth Bowl

Everyone on earth is scorched as the sun's heat gets stronger

[8]And the fourth angel poured out his vial upon the sun; and power was given unto him to scorch men with fire.

[9]And men were scorched with great heat, and blasphemed the name of God, which hath power over these plagues: and they repented not to give him glory.

The Fifth Bowl

The earth is made dark and all the people are tormented from their sores and pain

10And the fifth angel poured out his vial upon the seat of the beast; and his kingdom was full of darkness; and they gnawed their tongues for pain,

11And blasphemed the God of heaven because of their pains and their sores, and repented not of their deeds.

The Sixth Bowl

The Euphrates River goes dry, which allows armies from the east to march toward Jerusalem, heading for the Battle of Armageddon

12And the sixth angel poured out his vial upon the great river Euphrates; and the water thereof was dried up, that the way of the kings of the east might be prepared.

13And I saw three unclean spirits like frogs come out of the mouth of the dragon, and out of the mouth of the beast, and out of the mouth of the false prophet.

14For they are the spirits of devils, working miracles, which go forth unto the kings of the earth and of the whole world, to gather them to the battle of that great day of God Almighty.

[15]Behold, I come as a thief. Blessed is he that watcheth, and keepeth his garments, lest he walk naked, and they see his shame.

[16]And he gathered them together into a place called in the Hebrew tongue Armageddon.

The Seventh Bowl

The greatest earthquake ever hits the earth. Mountains fall, islands sink, and hailstones weighing over seventy pounds fall from the sky

[17]And the seventh angel poured out his vial into the air; and there came a great voice out of the temple of heaven, from the throne, saying, It is done.

[18]And there were voices, and thunders, and lightnings; and there was a great earthquake, such as was not since men were upon the earth, so mighty an earthquake, and so great.

[19]And the great city was divided into three parts, and the cities of the nations fell: and great Babylon came in remembrance before God, to give unto her the cup of the wine of the fierceness of his wrath.

[20]And every island fled away, and the mountains were not found.

[21]And there fell upon men a great hail out of heaven, every stone about the weight of a talent: and men blasphemed God because of the plague of the hail; for the plague thereof was exceeding great.

Not only do you have that to look forward to, but also what "man" is going to do while the judgments from God are being released upon this Earth.

But Jesus tells us:

Mathew 10

[28]And fear not them which kill the body, but are not able to kill the soul: but rather fear him which is able to destroy both soul and body in hell.

Revelation 7

[14]And I said unto him, Sir, thou knowest. And he said to me, These are they which came out of great tribulation, and have washed their robes, and made them white in the blood of the Lamb.

And in the end, the Beast has this to count on for he will NOT be the victor...

Revelation 19

[20]And the beast was taken, and with him the false prophet that wrought miracles before him, with which he deceived them that had received the mark of the beast, and them that worshipped his image. These both were cast alive into a lake of fire burning with brimstone.

As I finally complete this letter, the world is focused on one of many deceptions that have been created to confuse and divert people's attention from the truth. The Bible says:

Luke 21

[8]And he said, Take heed that ye be not deceived: for many shall come in my name, saying, "I am Christ; and the time draweth near: go ye not therefore after them."

Take a stand and don't follow the crowd (unless they are following Jesus). When someone says Jesus' image has been seen in a tree, or a dirty window, or please, a piece of toast—don't follow after them, instead follow the true Jesus.

John 14

[6]Jesus saith unto him, "I am the way, the truth, and the life: no man cometh unto the Father, but by me."

You don't have to take my word for all of this either…but read the Word for yourself; grab a Bible and read!

Although this little book contains scriptures to back up the statements that have been made, the Bible is the complete Word of God and it will answer all your questions if you just read it for yourself. The Bible also says:

Proverbs 2

[1]My son, if thou wilt receive my words, and hide my commandments with thee;

[2]So that thou incline thine ear unto wisdom, and apply thine heart to understanding;

[3]Yea, if thou criest after knowledge, and liftest up thy voice for understanding;

[4]If thou seekest her as silver, and searchest for her as for hid treasures;

[5]Then shalt thou understand the fear of the LORD, and find the knowledge of God.

[6]For the LORD giveth wisdom: out of his mouth cometh knowledge and understanding.

[7]He layeth up sound wisdom for the righteous: he is a buckler to them that walk uprightly.

[8]He keepeth the paths of judgment, and preserveth the way of his saints.

[9]Then shalt thou understand righteousness, and judgment, and equity; yea, every good path.

[10]When wisdom entereth into thine heart, and knowledge is pleasant unto thy soul;

[11]Discretion shall preserve thee, understanding shall keep thee:

[12]To deliver thee from the way of the evil man, from the man that speaketh froward things;

[13]Who leave the paths of uprightness, to walk in the ways of darkness;

[14]Who rejoice to do evil, and delight in the frowardness of the wicked;

[15]Whose ways are crooked, and they are froward in their paths:

[16]To deliver thee from the strange woman, even from the stranger which flattereth with her words;

[17]Which forsaketh the guide of her youth, and forgetteth the covenant of her God.

[18]For her house inclineth unto death, and her paths unto the dead.

[19]None that go unto her return again, neither take they hold of the paths of life.

[20]That thou mayest walk in the way of good men, and keep the paths of the righteous.

[21]For the upright shall dwell in the land, and the perfect shall remain in it.

[22]But the wicked shall be cut off from the earth, and the transgressors shall be rooted out of it.

It's been said that if you don't stand for something you'll fall for anything. Well, you've done your share of falling and *now* is the time to stand!

Take a stand for Jesus; take a stand for what's right...

Ephesians 6

[10]Finally, my brethren, be strong in the Lord, and in the power of his might.

[11]Put on the whole armour of God, that ye may be able to stand against the wiles of the devil.

[12]For we wrestle not against flesh and blood, but against principalities, against powers, against the rulers of the darkness of this world, against spiritual wickedness in high places.

[13]Wherefore take unto you the whole armour of God, that ye may be able to withstand in the evil day, and having done all, to stand.

At this time you still have hope. Ask Jesus to forgive you and cleanse you of your sins, and to come into your heart and to be the ruler of it now and forever. Denounce the Beast and take a stand no matter what the bodily cost. Although you may still lose your life, your soul will not be lost. You will have all of eternity to look forward to instead of endure.

If you believe what you have read in this book, and you want to accept the salvation that Jesus so freely offers, pray the following prayer:

God, I accept that Jesus is your Son and that He was born of the Virgin Mary. I believe that He died on the cross, that His blood was shed for my sins, and that He arose from the dead. I know that I have disobeyed you and have not lived the way you would have me to live. I ask you to forgive me of my sins. I now ask Jesus to come into my heart. Be my Savior, Lord of my life and soon coming King. Help me to follow your example and to live the rest of my life for you. In Jesus' name I ask these things, and in faith I accept my salvation and new life in you. Amen.

If you have read this and still are not convinced that Jesus is the way, the way to life, the way to live…and die, just remember when all of this is over and you're asked why you turned him away, you can't say no one ever told you the truth.

> May God keep your soul until
> Jesus returns in victory
> *—and* us with Him!

Revelation 22

[17]And the Spirit and the bride say, "Come." And let him that heareth say, "Come." And let him that is athirst come. And whosoever will, let him take the water of life freely.

ONLY A MOMENT AGO

Only a moment ago
The world had people of God.
Only a moment ago
You could have walked where angels trod.

Only a moment ago
A man stood knocking at your door.
Only a moment ago
He was gone and is now standing with the Lord.

Only a moment ago
He came, and now for you it may be too late.
Only a moment ago
He came, and it may have cost your soul to wait.

Only a moment ago
I traded a lie for the truth.
Only a moment ago
I would have been left behind...like you.

ONE BELIEVER'S TESTIMONY

How Did You Come To Know The Lord?

Where Did God Bring You Out Of Or Deliver You From?

Where Would You Be Now If God Had Not Saved You?

How Is Your Life Different Now?

How Has God Blessed You?

Have You Felt God Directing You To Do Something You Weren't Sure Of, But You Knew He Was Leading You?

What Are You Looking Forward To In Heaven And Eternity?

Since You Were "Saved," Have You Ever Wanted To Go Back To Your "Old Life"?

Is There Anything Worth More Than God?

Message From A Raptured Soul

CPSIA information can be obtained at www.ICGtesting.com
Printed in the USA
BVOW05s0502131014

370381BV00001B/8/P